بِسْمِ اللَّهِ الرَّحْمَٰنِ الرَّحِيمِ

In the Name of Allah, The Most Gracious,
The Most Merciful.

Disclaimer

Contact: admin@islamiclessonsmadeeasy.com.au

Visit us:

- Facebook.com/islamiclessonsmadeeasy
- Youtube.com/islamiclessonsmadeeasy
- Instagram.com/islamic_lessons_me
- Islamiclessonsmadeeasy.com.au
- Ilme.net.au

The pictures used are the property of Islamic Lessons Made Easy. The content and rulings are taken from various leading scholars and are presented in a simplified manner. Therefore, for the exact definition and explanation, please refer to the original sources.

First Edition

Contents

Transliteration 4

Introduction 5

Ḥadīth 6

Essentials of Ḥajj 7

Items to take 12

Ḥajj Rituals 14

ʿUmrah al-Tamattuʿ 17

Ḥajj al-Tamattuʿ 41

Recommended Acts 69

Ṭawāf al-Wadāʿ 72

Medina 74

Glossary 76

Transliteration

ا	a
ب	b
ت	t
ث	th
ج	j
ح	ḥ
خ	kh
د	d
ذ	dh
ر	r
ز	z
س	s
ش	sh
ص	ṣ
ض	ḍ
ط	ṭ
ظ	ẓ
ع	ʿ
غ	gh
ف	f
ق	q
ك	k
ل	l
م	m
ن	n
ه	h
و	w
ي	y
ىٰ / آ / ـَـا	ā
ـِـي	ī
ـُـو	ū

ʾ - Read with a sudden pause of air.

(n) - It's best not to pronounce it. But if you do, skip the letter that follows it.

صلى الله عليه وآله وسلم - Blessings of Allah be upon him and his family.

عليه السلام - Peace be upon him.

عليهم السلام - Peace be upon them.

سبحانه وتعالى - Glorious and Exalted Is He.

Introduction

Ḥajj is one of the fundamental branches of Islam, obligatory for all Muslims who are physically and financially able to perform it. Failing to perform Ḥajj when capable is considered a major sin and denying its obligation is regarded as disbelief.

Ḥajj is more than a physical journey, it's a profound spiritual experience that signifies a Muslim's submission to Allah ﷻ. It is a time for worship, reflection and personal transformation which is performed in Mecca during the Islamic month of Dhul-Ḥijjah.

The pilgrimage is rooted in the story of Prophet Ibrāhīm عليه السلام, his wife Hājar and their son Prophet Ismāʿīl عليه السلام, who all demonstrated unwavering faith and obedience to Allah ﷻ. The rituals of Ḥajj reflect their trials and carry deep spiritual lessons on faith, trust in Allah ﷻ and overcoming life's greatest challenges.

Ḥajj is a transformative journey designed to deepen a Muslim's relationship with Allah ﷻ. It reminds believers of their true purpose: to worship Allah ﷻ, live in submission to Him and seek His forgiveness. It offers a unique opportunity for self-reflection, repentance and spiritual renewal.

During Ḥajj, pilgrims experience profound humility, realising that in the vastness of Allah's creation, worldly achievements and status hold little significance. For many, completing Ḥajj feels like a spiritual rebirth, renewing their sense of purpose and strengthening their connection to Allah ﷻ.

Hadith

The Prophet ﷺ:

مَن سَوّفَ الحَجَّ حتّى يَموتَ بَعثَهُ الله يَومَ القِيامَةِ يَهودِيّاً أو نَصْرانيّاً.

Whoever intentionally delays their Ḥajj pilgrimage and dies without fulfilling it, Allah will resurrect them on the Day of Resurrection as a Jew or Christian (i.e., as a non-Muslim).

(*Biḥār al-Anwār*)

Imām Ja'far al-Ṣādiq ﵇:

مَن ماتَ في طريقِ مَكّةَ ذاهِباً أو جائياً، أمِنَ مِن الفَزَعِ الأكْبَرِ يَومَ القِيامَةِ.

Whoever dies on the road to Mecca (for Ḥajj), on the way there or back, will be safe from the Great Terror on the Day of Resurrection.

(*Al-Kāfī*)

Imām 'Alī ﵇:

الحاجُّ والمُعْتَمِرُ وفْدُ الله ويَحْبوهُ بالمَغفِرَةِ.

Those who go to Mecca for obligatory and voluntary pilgrimage are the envoys of Allah and His gift to them is forgiveness.

(*Al-Khiṣāl*)

Imām Ja'far al-Ṣādiq ﵇:

ما رأيتُ شَيئا أسْرَعَ غِنىً ولا أنْفى للفَقرِ مِن إدْمانِ حَجِّ هذا البَيتِ.

I have never seen anything faster at attracting wealth and at repelling poverty than habitual pilgrimage (Ḥajj) to this house.

(*Al-Amālī*)

ESSENTIALS OF HAJJ

The Obligation of Hajj

Every year, millions of Muslims from around the world undertake Ḥajj, the sacred pilgrimage of Islam, in Mecca, Saudi Arabia, during the Islamic month of Dhul-Ḥijjah.

Ḥajj is an obligation that you must perform at least once in your lifetime if you meet the necessary conditions. The duty to perform Ḥajj becomes binding as soon as these conditions are met.

If you delay performing Ḥajj without a valid reason after it becomes obligatory, you must fulfill the obligation in the following year until the pilgrimage is completed. Delaying Ḥajj without a legitimate reason is considered a major sin in Islam.

Once the obligation is established, it is crucial for you to make timely travel arrangements to ensure the pilgrimage is completed within the prescribed period.

Requirements for Hajj

The following requirements must be met for Ḥajj to be compulsory:

- You must have reached the age of Islamic maturity.
- You must be sane; an insane person is not required to perform the pilgrimage.
- You need enough time to travel to Mecca and complete all the required rituals. If you don't have sufficient time, it's not obligatory for you to go. In that case, you should save the money for the journey and plan to go the following year.
- You must have the health and strength to travel. If you cannot travel due to illness or old age, it's not obligatory for you to go personally. Instead, you should appoint someone to perform the pilgrimage on your behalf.
- The route must be safe, with no threat to your life, property or honour. If there is danger, Ḥajj is not obligatory.
- You must have enough funds to cover the expenses of the journey, including food, drink and other necessities. This also includes transportation for the return trip if you plan to return home. Additionally, you must be able to support yourself and your family on the return trip.

Preparation for Hajj

Before embarking on the journey for Ḥajj, you should:

Settle Debts: Ensure that all debts are cleared prior to departure. If repayment is not feasible, seek permission from creditors to defer payment until after returning.

Ensure Clean Funds: Make sure that the financial resources used for Ḥajj come from *ḥalāl* (permissible) earnings, ensuring they are free from any *ḥarām* (prohibited) earnings.

Pay Khums and Zakāh: Fulfill all obligatory religious dues, such as *Khums* and *Zakāh*, ensuring they are fully paid before commencing your journey.

Prepare a Will: Write a will to address any potential unforeseen events, including the possibility of death during the journey. Inform a trusted individual, who will not be traveling with you, of its location.

Seek Forgiveness: Ask for forgiveness from family, friends and anyone you may have wronged, to embark on Ḥajj with a clear conscience and pure heart.

Debts

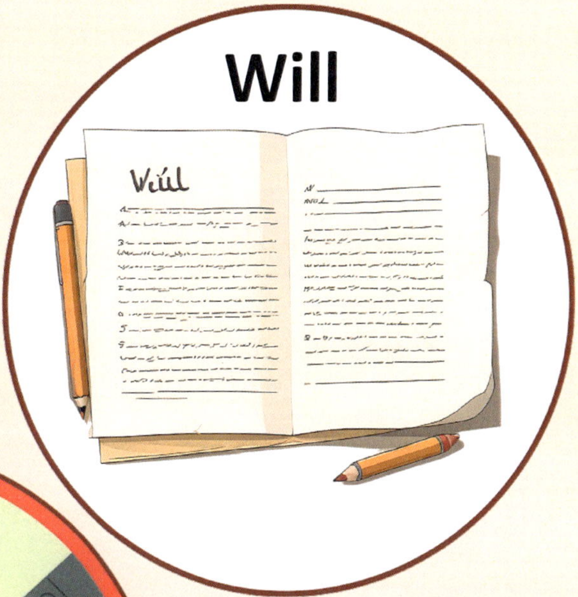
Will

Ḥarām

Forgive

Khums

Items to Take

- Valid passport with Ḥajj visa
- Vaccination records, especially for Meningitis
- Emergency contact details for urgent situations
- Prescribed medications and basic remedies
- Unscented soap, shampoo and toiletries
- Comfortable, breathable footwear
- Sandals for men that don’t cover the whole foot
- Small towel for hygiene
- Toothbrush and toothpaste
- Money belt for cash and important items
- Two pieces of unstitched cloths (*iḥrām*)* for males
- Long and modest clothing for women
- Supplication books or apps for specific prayers
- Qurān for reading
- *Turbah* for prostration in prayers
- Light blanket or sleeping bag for overnight stays in certain areas

*Refer to pg. 23

PASSPORT
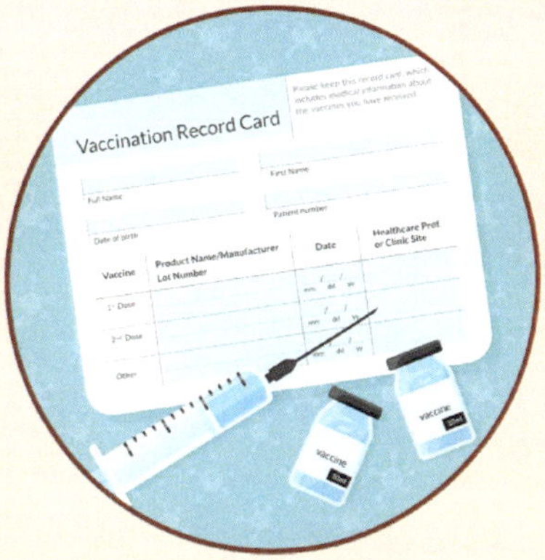
Vaccination Record Card

EMERGENCY
CALL
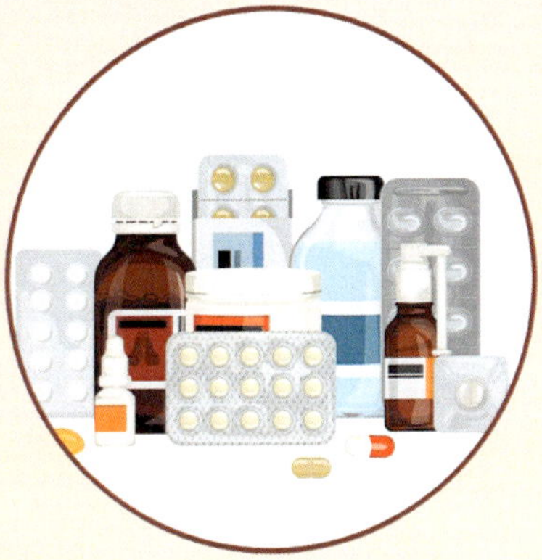
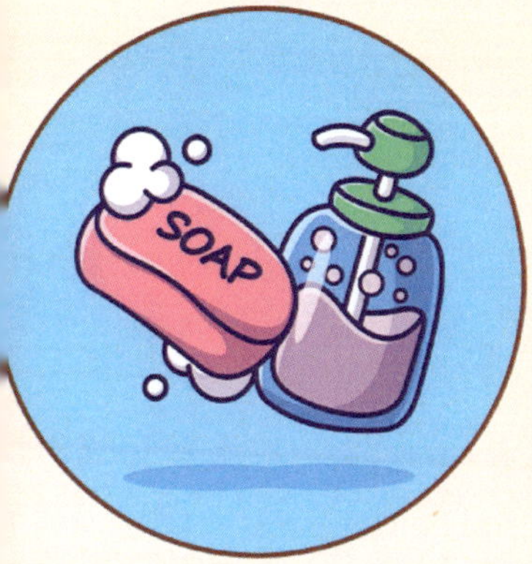
SOAP

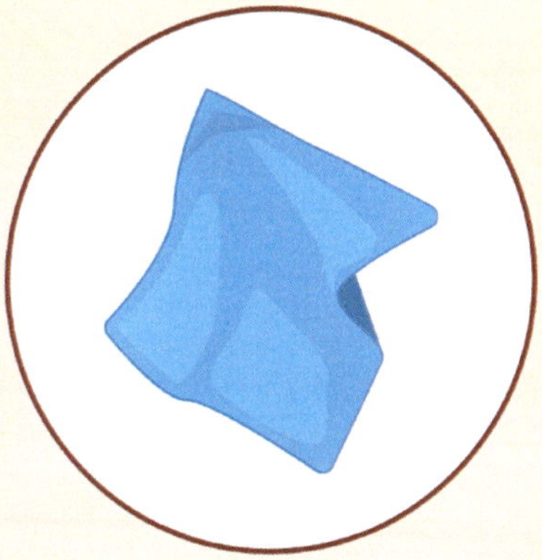
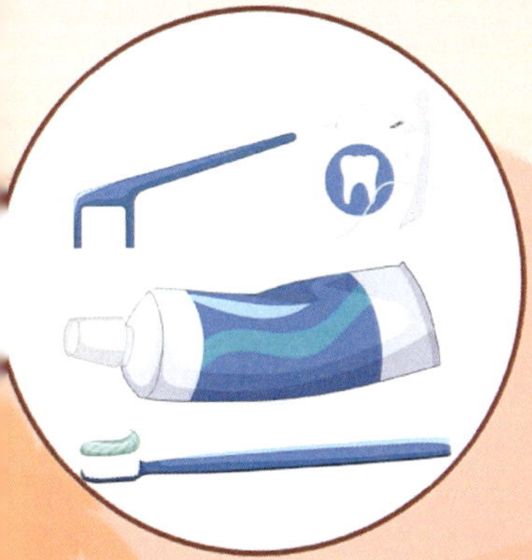
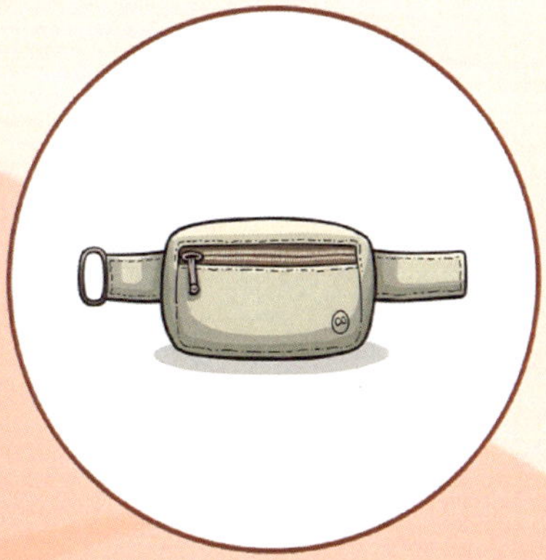

HAJJ RITUALS

Types of Hajj

- **Ḥajj al-Ifrād**: This type of Ḥajj is usually for residents of Mecca or those living within a 77km radius and is independent of ʿUmrah.

- **Ḥajj al-Qirān**: Similar to Ḥajj al-Ifrād, this type of Ḥajj is also usually for residents within the same geographic boundary. However, it differs in that the pilgrim must bring a sacrificial animal with them when entering the state of *iḥrām*.

- **Ḥajj al-Tamattuʿ**: This type of Ḥajj is performed by pilgrims from outside the Meccan region. It consists of two separate acts of worship: ʿUmrah al-Tamattuʿ, followed by Ḥajj al-Tamattuʿ. It is obligatory for ʿUmrah to be performed before Ḥajj, and both must take place during the same pilgrimage season.

We will be focusing on Ḥajj al-Tamattuʿ in this book, as it is the type of Ḥajj performed by most pilgrims.

Conditions for Hajj al-Tamattuʿ

- **Intention**: One must firmly intend to perform Ḥajj al-Tamattuʿ. If a different type of pilgrimage is intended, or if there is uncertainty in one's intention, the validity of the Ḥajj al-Tamattuʿ becomes invalid.

- **Succession**: Both ʿUmrah and Ḥajj must be performed during the designated Ḥajj season. ʿUmrah al-Tamattuʿ must occur in the months of Shawwāl, Dhul-Qaʿdah and Dhul-Ḥijjah. If any part of the ʿUmrah is performed before Shawwāl, the ʿUmrah becomes invalid for Ḥajj al-Tamattuʿ. Ḥajj al-Tamattuʿ occurs in Dhul-Ḥijjah.

- **Same Year Requirement**: The ʿUmrah and Ḥajj must be performed within the same year. If the ʿUmrah is completed but the Ḥajj is postponed to the following year, the Ḥajj al-Tamattuʿ becomes invalid.

‘UMRAH AL-TAMATTU‘

ʿUmrah al-Tamattuʿ

As previously mentioned, a person intending to perform Ḥajj al-Tamattuʿ must first complete ʿUmrah al-Tamattuʿ.

ʿUmrah al-Tamattuʿ consists of five actions:

- **Iḥrām:** Entering the state of *iḥrām* from the *mīqāt.*
- **Ṭawāf:** Performing seven rounds of circumambulation around the Kaʿbah.
- **Ṣalāt al-Ṭawāf:** Offering two *rakʿahs* of prayer behind Maqām Ibrāhīm عليه السلام.
- **Saʿy:** Walking seven times between *Ṣafāʾ* and *Marwah.*
- **Taqṣīr:** Cutting a portion of hair from the head, beard or moustache.

Upon completing these five acts, one exits the state of *iḥrām,* allowing most previously forbidden actions during *iḥrām* to become permissible once again.

ʿUmrah al-Tamattuʿ

Miqat

Mīqāt (literally meaning 'station') refers to the designated locations where pilgrims of Ḥajj or ʿUmrah wear their *iḥrām* clothing. Muslims who do not reside near Mecca must enter the state of *iḥrām* at one of the five specified *miqāt* locations before heading to the Kaʿbah.

The Five Miqāt locations are:

1. **Masjid al-Shajarah:** A historic mosque in Medina. Pilgrims departing from Medina put on their *iḥrām* here.

2. **Al-Juhfah:** Located between Mecca and Medina. This *miqāt* has a large mosque where thousands of pilgrims can put on their *iḥrām*.

3. **Wādī al-ʿAqīq:** This *miqāt* is divided into three areas: Maslakh, Qumrah and Dhat ʿIrq.

4. **Qarn al-Manāzil:** A mosque is situated here to accommodate pilgrims as they put on their *iḥrām*.

5. **Yalamlam:** This *miqāt* is located south of Mecca and serves pilgrims traveling from that direction.

Miqat

Medina
Masjid al-Shajarah
Wādī al-ʿAqīq
Al-Juhfah
Qarn al-Manāzil
Yalamlam

Recommended acts

Here are some recommended acts before putting on the *iḥrām*:

- Cleaning the body
- Clipping nails
- Trimming mustache
- Removing underarm hair and below the navel
- Growing the hair on the head and beard before shaving them during Ḥajj
- Performing *ghusl* at the *mīqāt* before putting on the *iḥrām* clothes
- Wearing cloths made of cotton for *iḥrām*
- Wearing the *iḥrām* after *Ẓuhr* prayer

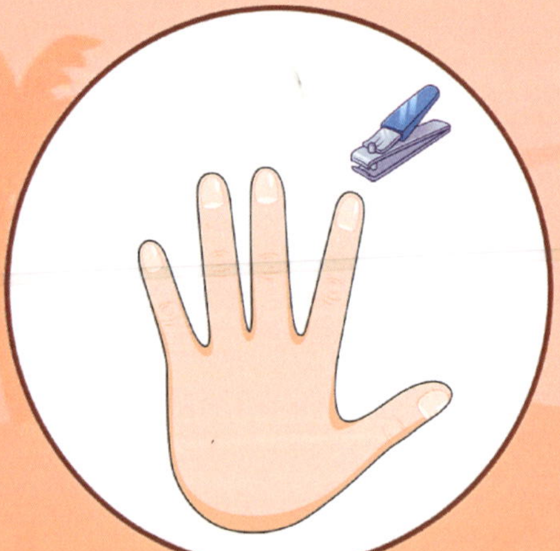

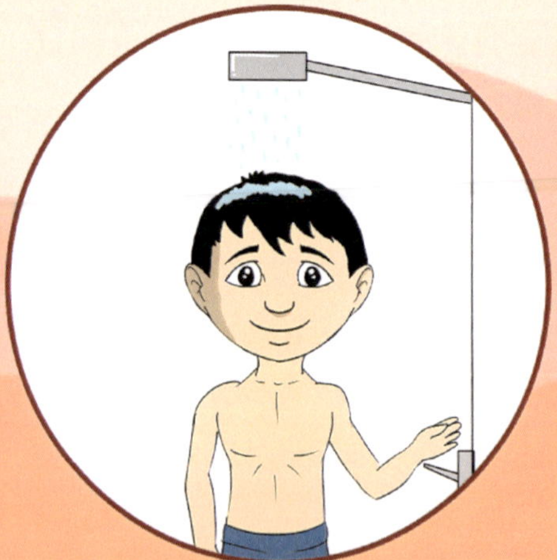

Ihram

At the *mīqāt*, three key obligations make the *iḥrām* valid:

- **Clothing:** The time to wear *iḥrām* is during the months of Shawwāl, Dhul-Qaʿdah and Dhul-Ḥijjah.

  Men must remove their day-to-day clothing and wear two unstitched garments. One of the garments must be wrapped around the waist covering from the navel to the knees. The second garment should cover both the shoulders, arms and a considerable part of the back.

  The garments must not be made of pure silk, gold or any material derived from animals. The garments should also be *ṭāhir* (ritually pure). It is preferred that the *iḥrām* be of white colour.

  Women do not share the same restriction as men regarding stitched clothing in the state of *iḥrām*. They are permitted to wear normal, modest clothing, with the exception of pure silk. It is also preferred that women wear a white *iḥrām*.

  If either of the garments becomes *najis* (ritually impure), it must be changed or rendered *ṭāhir* as soon as possible.

- **Intention:** The intention is to attain proximity to Allah ﷻ. It is not necessary for the intention to be uttered loudly.

- ***Talbiyah***: It consists of some specific phrases. Refer to page 24.

Talbiyah

Every pilgrim must recite these phrases of the *talbiyah* correctly. The *iḥrām* is not complete without the *talbiyah*. The most common phrases recited for the *talbiyah* are as follows:

لَبَّيكَ اَللّٰهُمَّ لَبَّيك، لَبَّيك لاشَريكَ لَكَ لَبَّيك، إنَّ الْحَمْدَ وَ النِّعْمَةَ لَكَ وَالْمُلك، لاشَريكَ لَكَ لَبَّيكَ

Labbayk Allāhumma labbayk, labbayka lā sharīka laka labayk, innal ḥamda wan-niʿmata laka wal mulk, lā sharīka laka labbayk

Here I am, O Allah, here I am, responding to Your call again and again. You have no partner. Indeed, all praise, blessings and sovereignty belong to You. You have no partner. Here I am responding to Your call.

As soon as the *talbiyah* has been recited, the pilgrim is now called a *muḥrim* until the *ʿUmrah* is over. Being a *muḥrim* comes with certain restrictions, as there are specific actions and things that become forbidden while in this sacred state.

Intention
Talbiyah
Two unstitched garments
Intention
Talbiyah
Modest clothing

Prohibitions during Ihram

Certain acts are prohibited during the state of *iḥrām*:

- Hunting
- Lying, boasting or swearing
- Carrying weapons
- Cutting nails
- Extracting teeth
- Engaging in marriage contracts
- Using perfumes
- Applying oil to the body
- Removing hair from the body
- Applying *kuḥl* (eye cosmetic) for both men and women
- Killing insects that live on the human body, like lice
- Self-beautification, such as wearing jewellery or ornaments
- Looking in the mirror for the purpose of beautification
- Removing blood from the body, such as through cupping or blood donation
- Sexual activities including: intercourse, touching, kissing or looking at others with lust
- Engaging in disputes or quarrels, especially those involving swearing by Allah ﷻ
- **For women:** covering the face with a veil or wearing gloves
- **For men:** wearing shoes or socks that cover the entire foot, covering the head or immersing it in water, wearing sewn clothes, staying under artificial shade (e.g., umbrellas, the roof of a vehicle); natural shade, like that of trees or clouds, is permissible.

If any of these prohibitions are acted upon, there are specific *kaffārahs* (atonements) attached, such as sacrificing a camel, cow, or sheep, paying a monetary penalty or fasting.

Prohibitions during Ihram

Recommended acts

Here are some recommended acts when entering the *Ḥaram* (sacred precincts that surround the Kaʿbah):

- Performing *Ghusl* before entering Mecca and enter with calmness and dignity.
- Chewing a bit of the aromatic grass known as *'Idhkhir'* upon entering the *Ḥaram.*
- Entering the mosque barefoot through Bab al-Salām (The Gate of Peace).
- Standing at the entrance of the mosque and recite supplications.
- Entering the mosque facing the Kaʿbah.
- Touching and kissing the Black Stone.
- Sending blessings upon the Prophet ﷺ and his family عليهم السلام.

For each of these actions, specific supplications are recited and can be found in supplication books.

اللّٰهُمَّ صَلِّ عَلَى مُحَمَّدٍ وَآلِ مُحَمَّدٍ
Allahumma ṣalli ʿala
Muḥammadi(n)w wa āli
Muḥammad

Preconditions of Tawaf

In ʿUmrah al-Tamattuʿ, the second obligation is *ṭawāf*. Several preconditions must be met for the proper performance of *ṭawāf*:

- **Intention:** You must make the intention for *ṭawāf* with the purpose of seeking closeness to Allah ﷻ, specifically for ʿUmrah al-Tamattuʿ.
- **Purity:** You must be free from major impurities such as menstruation and *janābah.* You must also be free from minor impurities, meaning you should perform *wuḍūʾ* after using the toilet or passing gas.
- **Body and Clothing:** Your body, clothing and *iḥrām* must be clean and free from any physical impurities such as blood, urine, etc.
- **Circumcision:** If you are male, you must be circumcised before performing *ṭawāf.*
- **Wuḍūʾ:** You must be in a state of *wuḍūʾ* throughout the performance of *ṭawāf.*

Performance of Tawaf

- To perform *ṭawāf*, one must circumambulate the Kaʿbah seven times in a counterclockwise direction with the intention of *ṭawāf*.
- The *ṭawāf* begins and ends at the Black Stone. In the final round, it is recommended to continue slightly past the Black Stone to ensure the completion of the seven rounds.
- During *ṭawāf*, your left shoulder should always be directed toward the Kaʿbah. While you may move your face left or right, your left shoulder must consistently point towards the Kaʿbah.
- Ḥijr Ismāʿīl must be included in the *ṭawāf*, meaning you must circumambulate around it without entering the area or climbing its walls.
- It is preferred that the *ṭawāf* should be performed between the Kaʿbah and Maqām Ibrāhīm.
- Seven continuous rounds are required for *ṭawāf*, and the rounds must follow one another without significant interruption.

Performance of Tawaf

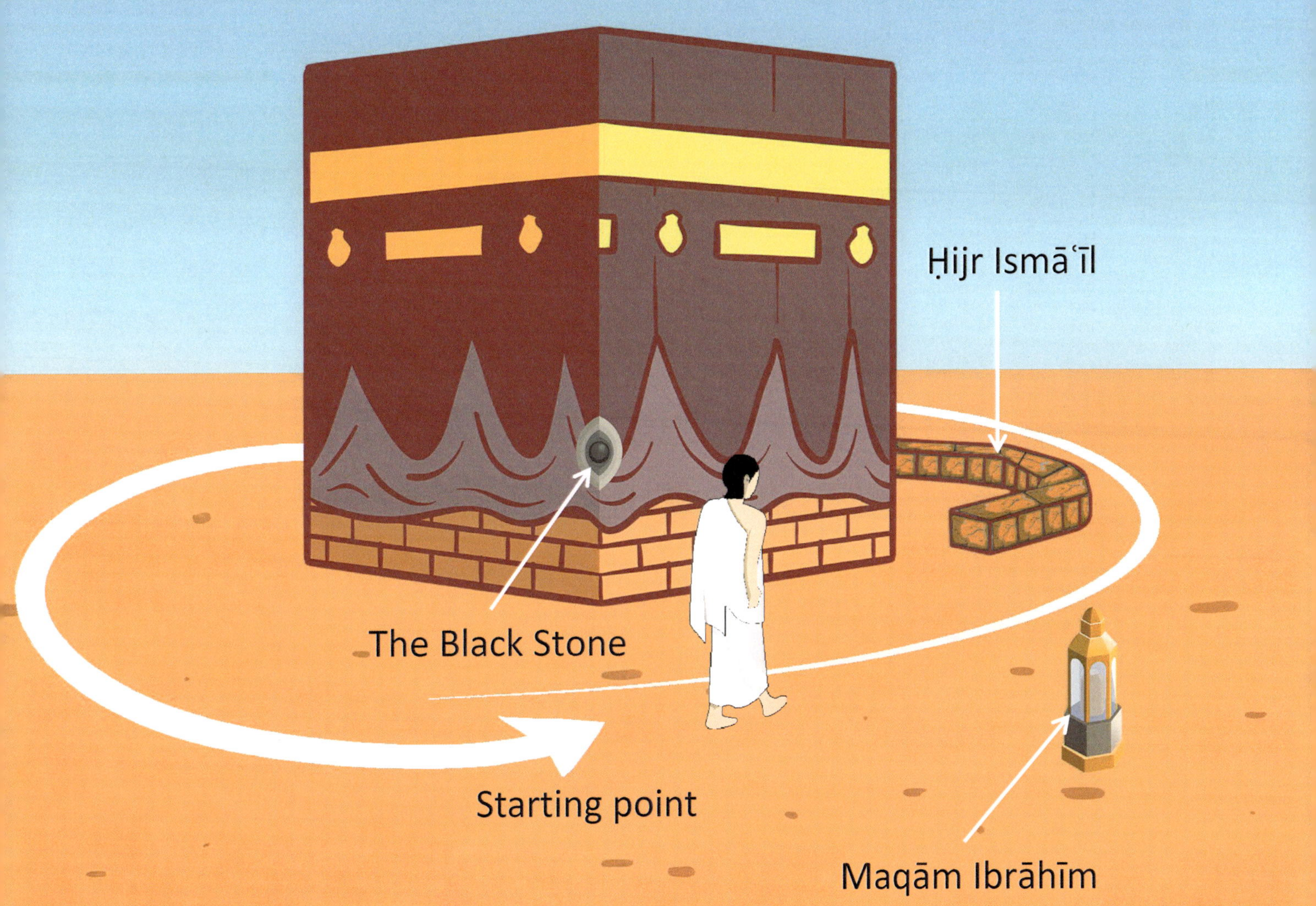

Salat al-Tawaf

The third obligation in ʿUmrah al-Tamattuʿ is to perform two *rakʿahs* of prayer after completing *ṭawāf.*

- The intention should be to seek nearness to Allah: "I am praying two *rakʿahs* of Ṣalāt al-Ṭawāf for ʿUmrah al-Tamattuʿ seeking nearness to Allah."

- The prayer should be performed immediately after *ṭawāf* without unnecessary delay.

- This prayer resembles the *Fajr* prayer, with the option to recite it aloud or quietly. It is recommended to recite Sūrah Al-Ikhlāṣ in the first *rakʿah* after Sūrah Al-Fātiḥah, and Sūrah Al-Kāfirūn in the second *rakʿah*. After completing the prayer, you should praise and thank Allah, send blessings on the Prophet and his family and ask Allah to accept your prayer.

- It is obligatory to perform this prayer near Maqām Ibrāhīm, specifically behind it.

- If performing the two *rakʿahs* directly behind Maqām Ibrāhīm is not possible due to crowding or other obstacles, you may perform the prayer on either side of the Maqām, as long as you remain in its general vicinity. This means you can be slightly to the right or left, provided you stay behind the Maqām in relation to the Kaʿbah.

- If necessary, you may perform the prayer further away from Maqām Ibrāhīm, as long as you remain behind it.

Salat al-Tawaf

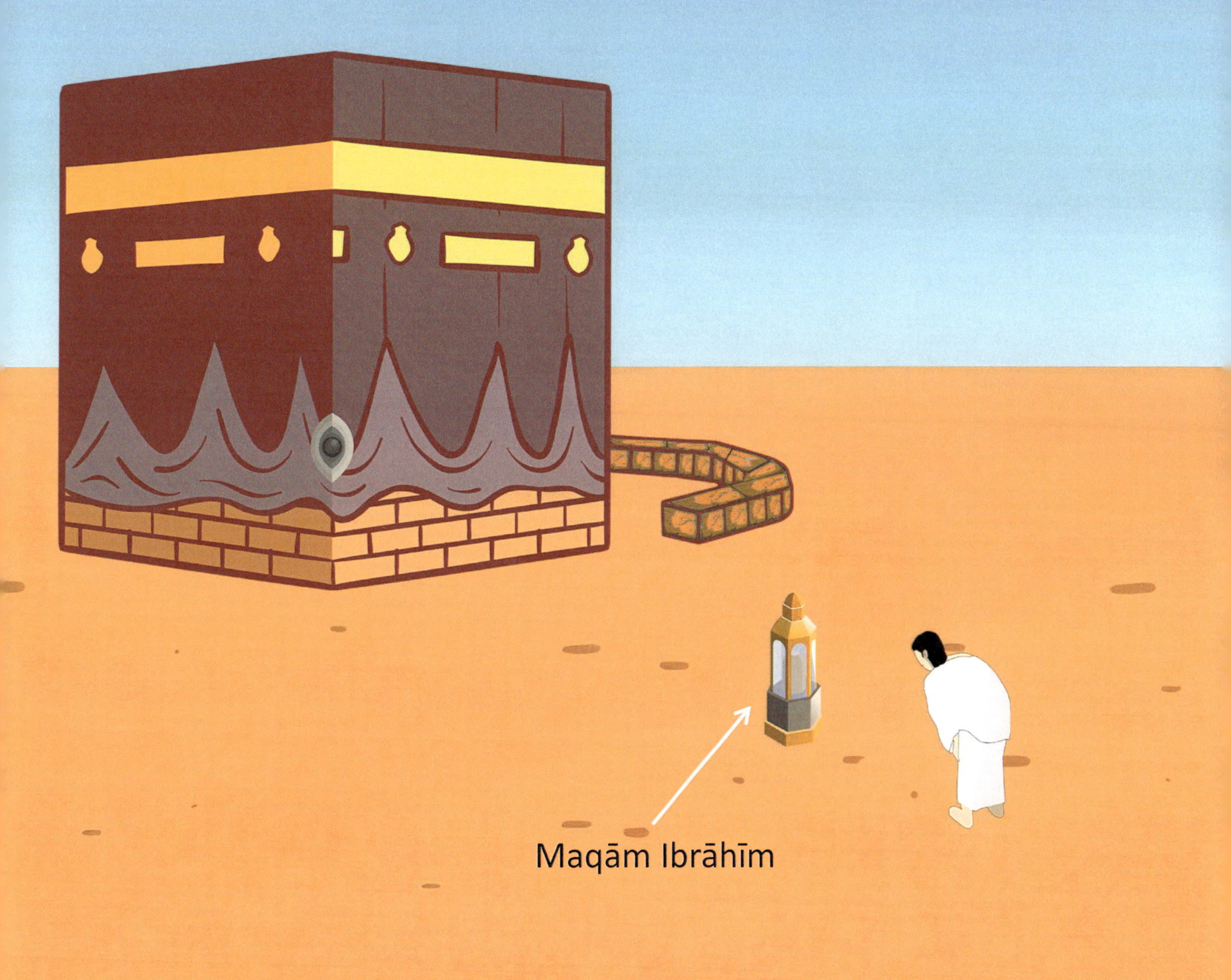

Sa'y

The fourth obligation of 'Umrah al-Tamattu' is performing *sa'y* between the two small rises, Ṣafā and Marwah.

Although these were once full mountains, over time, both have been significantly reduced in size due to the construction of Masjid al-Ḥarām and are now enclosed within the modern structure of the Mosque.

- During *sa'y*, it is obligatory to have the intention of seeking nearness to Allah ﷻ.
- *Sa'y* must be performed after completing *ṭawāf* and its accompanying prayer. If done before either, it must be repeated after both are completed.
- *Sa'y* consists of seven alternating laps, starting from Ṣafā and ending at Marwah.
- Walking is preferable, with brisk walking recommended on the designated path. Walking in a straight line is not necessary.
- While walking, you should face Marwah when heading towards it, and Ṣafā when heading back.
- The sequence of laps should be followed, though it is permissible to rest at Ṣafā, Marwah or between them. Breaks should only be taken when necessary, such as due to fatigue or for prayer.

Sa'y

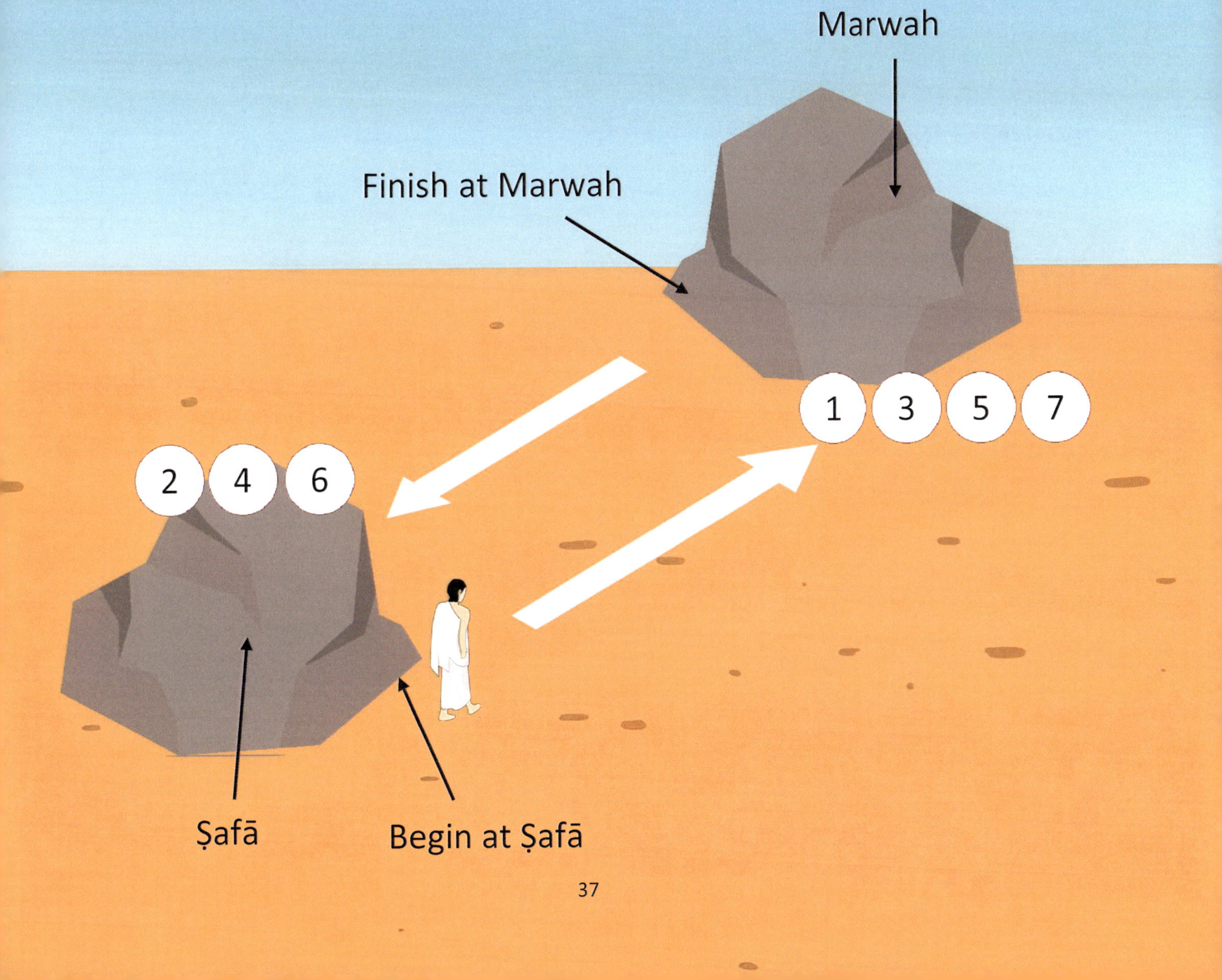

Taqsir

The fifth obligation of ʿUmrah al-Tamattuʿ is *taqṣīr.*

- You must perform it with the intention of seeking nearness to Allah ﷻ.
- *Taqṣīr* involves cutting a small amount of hair from your head, beard or mustache. Simply plucking hair is not enough and shaving your head is forbidden.
- You must perform *taqṣīr* after *saʿy,* it is not permissible to do it before completing *saʿy.*
- *Taqṣīr* does not need to be done immediately after *saʿy*, and you can perform it wherever you prefer, whether at the *saʿy* location, at home or elsewhere.
- If you deliberately fail to perform *taqṣīr* and then enter *iḥrām* for Ḥajj, your ʿUmrah will be invalid.
- Once you complete *taqṣīr* in ʿUmrah al-Tamattuʿ, all the prohibitions of *iḥrām* are lifted, except for the prohibition on shaving your head.

Taqsir

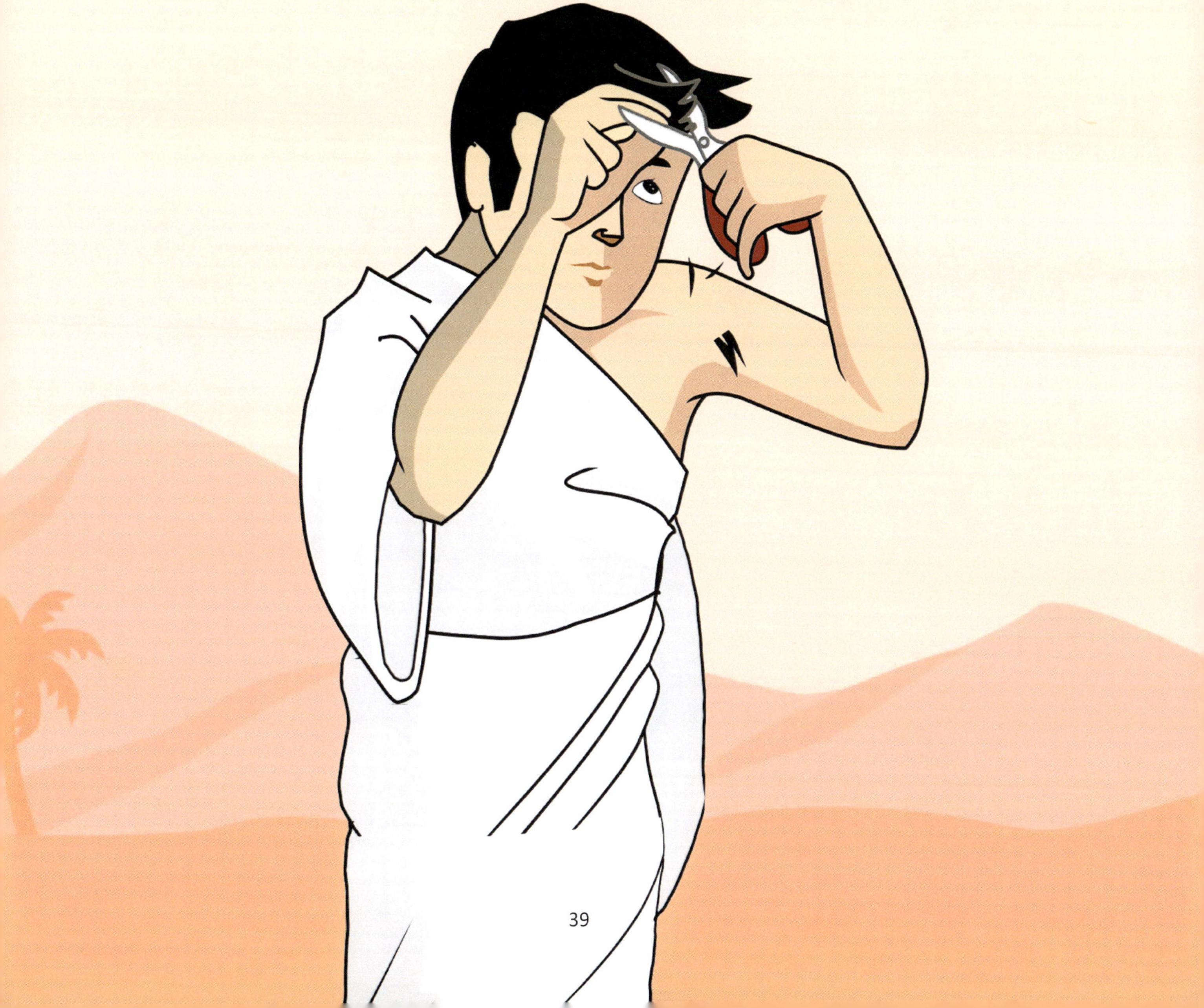

CONGRATULATIONS!

You have completed
'Umrah al-Tammatu'

HAJJ AL-TAMATTUʿ

Ḥajj al-Tamattuʿ

After completing ʿUmrah al-Tamattuʿ, it is time to perform Ḥajj al-Tamattuʿ which consists of 13 essential actions:

1. Wearing the *iḥrām* in Mecca.
2. Staying at ʿArafah.
3. Spending the night in Muzdalifah (Mashʿar al-Ḥarām).
4. Stoning Jamarah al-ʿAqabah (the large pillar symbolising Satan).
5. Sacrificing an animal.
6. Shaving (*ḥalq*) or trimming (*taqṣīr*) the hair.
7. Performing *ṭawāf* of Ḥajj.
8. Praying Ṣalāt al-Ṭawāf of Ḥajj behind Maqām Ibrāhīm.
9. Performing *Saʿy* between Ṣafā and Marwah.
10. Performing Ṭawāf al-Nisāʾ.
11. Praying Ṣalāt al-Ṭawāf al-Nisāʾ behind Maqām Ibrāhīm.
12. Spending the nights in Minā.
13. Stoning all three Jamarāt (first, middle and large pillars symbolising Satan).

Hajj al-Tamattuʿ

Ihram for Hajj

The first obligation for Ḥajj al-Tammatu' is to put on the *iḥrām*. There are certain conditions for your *iḥrām* to be valid:

Intention: Your intention should be to wear the *iḥrām* for Ḥajj al-Tammatu', seeking closeness to Allah ﷻ.

Talbiyah: Reciting the *talbiyah* correctly is essential, as the *iḥrām* is not complete without it. (Refer to page 24 for details).

Timing of Iḥrām: The best time to wear *iḥrām* is on the 8th of Dhul-Ḥijjah at *Ẓuhr* time. Elderly or sick people who fear overcrowding may wear it up to three days earlier.

Iḥrām Restrictions: You cannot wear *iḥrām* for Ḥajj until you have completed *taqṣīr* in 'Umrah al-Tamattu'.

Iḥrām Rules: The rules and prohibitions of *iḥrām* for Ḥajj are the same as those for 'Umrah. (Refer to page 26 for details).

Iḥrām Location: It is obligatory to wear *iḥrām* in Mecca, ideally from Masjid al-Ḥarām. It's recommended to pray a two *rak'ah* prayer at Maqām Ibrāhīm or Ḥijr Ismā'īl before putting on the *iḥrām*.

Forgetting Iḥrām: If you forget to wear *iḥrām* due to ignorance or an oversight, you must return to Mecca to put it on, even if you've reached 'Arafah. If it's not possible, you should wear it wherever you are.

Ihram

Intention
Talbiyah
Intention
Talbiyah
Two unsewn garments
Modest clothing

ʿArafah

The second obligation of Ḥajj al-Tamattuʿ is to stay at ʿArafah on the 9th of Dhul-Ḥijjah.

- This is a day of immense spiritual significance where millions of pilgrims gather at the plain of ʿArafah, standing in humility before their Creator. Beyond its significance in the pilgrimage, this day is marked by Allah's abundant mercy and forgiveness, offering all believers a unique opportunity to seek closeness to Him.

- For Ḥajj al-Tamattuʿ you must arrive at ʿArafah before *Ẓuhr* with the intention of staying from *Ẓuhr* until *Maghrib* in obedience to Allah's command. It is obligatory to remain within the boundaries of ʿArafah during this period.

- It is highly recommended to engage in prayer, supplication and other acts of worship while staying at ʿArafah, maximising this precious time. After sunset you should leave ʿArafah and proceed to Muzdalifah.

Minā
Mecca
Night
Muzdalifah
Day
ʿArafah

Recommended acts in ʿArafah

- Staying on the left side of Mount Raḥmah on level ground.
- Remaining in a state of ritual purity and performing *ghusl* before your stay.
- Avoiding distractions that take away attention from acts of worship.
- Performing *Ẓuhr* and *ʿAṣr* prayers together at their prime time.
- Praying and beseeching Allah ﷻ as much as possible.
- Reflecting on one's sins and sincerely seeking forgiveness.
- Weeping or becoming tearful out of sincerity and devotion.
- Facing the *Qiblah* while praising, thanking and glorifying Allah ﷻ.
- Praying for oneself, parents and fellow believers.
- Reciting supplication number 47 from *Al-Ṣaḥīfa al-Sajjādīyya.*
- Reciting the supplication of Imām Ḥusayn عليه السلام found in books like *Mafātīḥ al-Jinān.*

Mount Raḥmah

Muzdalifah

The third obligation of Ḥajj al-Tamattuʿ is the stay at Muzdalifah, also known as Mashʿar al-Ḥarām. This stay occurs immediately after leaving ʿArafah.

- When *Maghrib* time enters while you are at ʿArafah, you should proceed to Muzdalifah and spend a part of the night there until *Fajr* on the 10th of Dhul-Ḥijjah (Eid al-Aḍḥā). As a precaution you should stay until sunrise.

- Exceptions are made for women, children, the elderly, the sick, the weak, the fearful and those responsible for them. They are allowed to stay for part of the night and leave Muzdalifah to proceed to Minā before *Fajr*.

- You should make the intention to stay in Muzdalifah as part of Ḥajj al-Tamattuʿ, seeking closeness to Allah ﷻ.

Muzdalifah

It is recommended to:

- Combine the *Maghrib* and *ʿIshāʾ* prayers in Muzdalifah.
- Collect 70 small pebbles from Muzdalifah for the stoning ritual in Minā.
- Engage in supplications and the remembrance of Allah ﷻ throughout the night.
- Remain humble, reflect on your journey and engage in worship.

Mina

On the 10th of Dhul-Ḥijjah, you must proceed from Muzdalifah towards Minā. In Minā, there are three essential acts to perform:

1. Throwing seven pebbles at the large pillar (Jamarah al-ʿAqabah) that symbolises Satan.

2. Sacrificing an animal in commemoration of the sacrifice of Prophet Ibrāhīm عليه السلام.

3. Shaving or trimming the hair as a symbol of purification.

After completing these three actions, most of the prohibitions during *iḥrām* are lifted, marking the transition to a state of partial release from the restrictions of the sacred state.

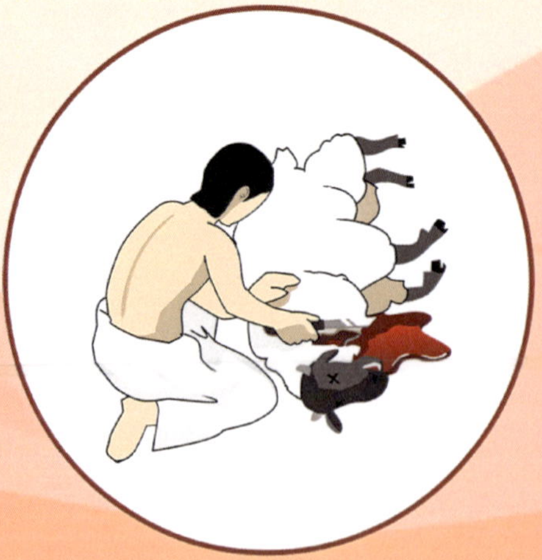

Proceed from Muzdalifah to Minā

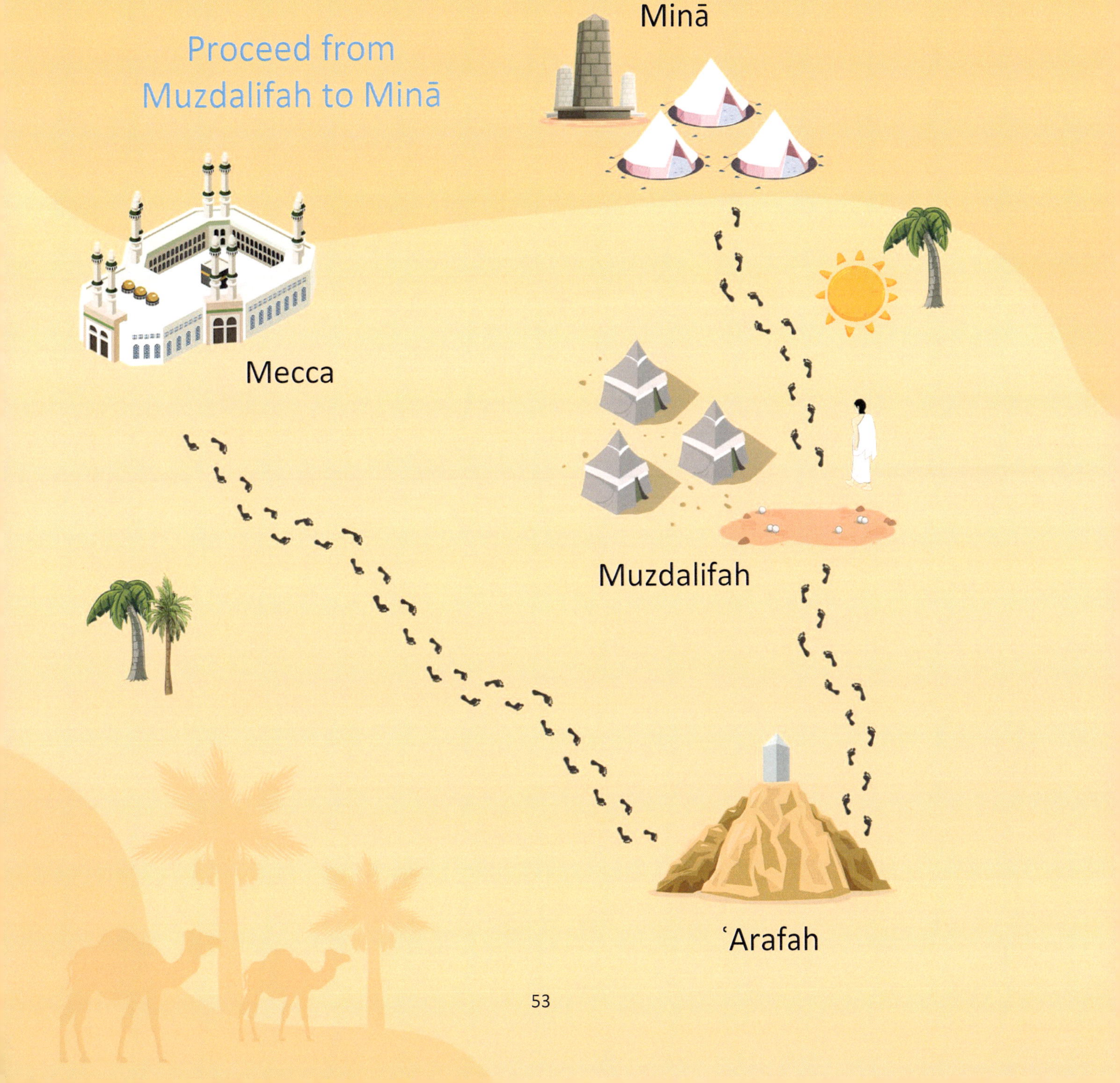

Jamarah al-ʿAqabah

In Minā the fourth obligation of Ḥajj al-Tamattuʿ is throwing seven pebbles at the large pillar that symbolisers Satan on the 10th of Dhul-Ḥijjah (Eid al-Aḍḥā).

Several conditions must be met:

- The act must be performed with the intention of seeking closeness to Allah ﷻ.
- Seven pebbles must be thrown - not any less.
- Only pebbles may be used - no other objects are valid.
- The pebbles must be thrown one at a time, throwing two or more at once is invalid.
- The pebbles must hit the large pillar, those that miss do not count.
- The pebbles must reach the pillar by being thrown, not placed on it.
- The pebbles must be thrown by hand; using the mouth, foot, or a tool (such as a slingshot) is invalid as a precaution.
- The stoning must occur between sunrise and *Maghrib* on Eid Day. However, women, the ill and those that were permitted to leave Muzdalifah at night may perform it at night.
- The pebbles must not have been used for stoning before.
- As a precaution, the pebbles must hit the original height of the pillar. Hitting the recent extensions or upper levels does not suffice.
- It is recommended that the pebbles be colored, marked, soft and roughly fingertip-sized. The person stoning should be standing and in a state of purity.

Jamarah al-'Aqabah

Sacrificing an Animal

After completing the stoning of Jamarah al-ʿAqaba in Minā, the fifth obligation of Ḥajj al-Tamattuʿ is the sacrifice of an animal.

Several conditions must be met:

- The act must be performed with the intention of seeking closeness to Allah ﷻ.
- The sacrifice must be offered during the day.
- It is an obligatory precaution that the sacrifice be performed after stoning the large pillar.
- The sacrifice must be made in Minā. If space or logistical constraints prevent this, it is permissible to offer the sacrifice outside Minā.
- Based on precaution, the sacrifice should be carried out on the 10th of Dhul-Ḥijjah (Eid al-Aḍḥā).
- The sacrificial animal must be a camel, cow or sheep that has reached a certain age. It must also be physically complete—animals that are blind, lame, have severed ears or broken internal horns are not valid.
- Each sacrificial animal is sufficient for one person.
- Iron or stainless-steel knives should be used for the sacrifice.
- You may perform the sacrifice personally or appoint an agent to do it on your behalf.

Sacrificing an Animal

Halq or Taqsir

After completing the sacrifice of an animal in Minā, the sixth obligation of Ḥajj al-Tamattuʿ is to trim or shave off the hair.

Several conditions must be met:

- The act must be performed with the intention of seeking closeness to Allah ﷻ.
- Based on obligatory precaution, cutting or shaving the hair should be done after stoning at Jamarah al-ʿAqaba and after slaughtering an animal.
- Shaving or shortening must be done in Minā.
- It is not permissible for women to shave their heads (*ḥalq)*, instead, they must shorten their hair (*taqṣīr*).
- Men may choose between shaving their heads or shortening their hair, though shaving is preferable. If you are performing Ḥajj for the first time, then based on obligatory precaution, you must shave your head.
- Based on precaution *ḥalq* or *taqṣīr* should not be postponed until the night.
- A person who wishes to shave another person's head cannot do so before performing their own *ḥalq* or *taqṣīr*.
- Once you shave or shorten your hair, everything forbidden to you during *iḥrām* becomes permissible, except for sexual activities, using perfumes and hunting.

Halq or Taqsir

It is recommended to start shaving from the right side and to bury the hair in your tent in Minā.

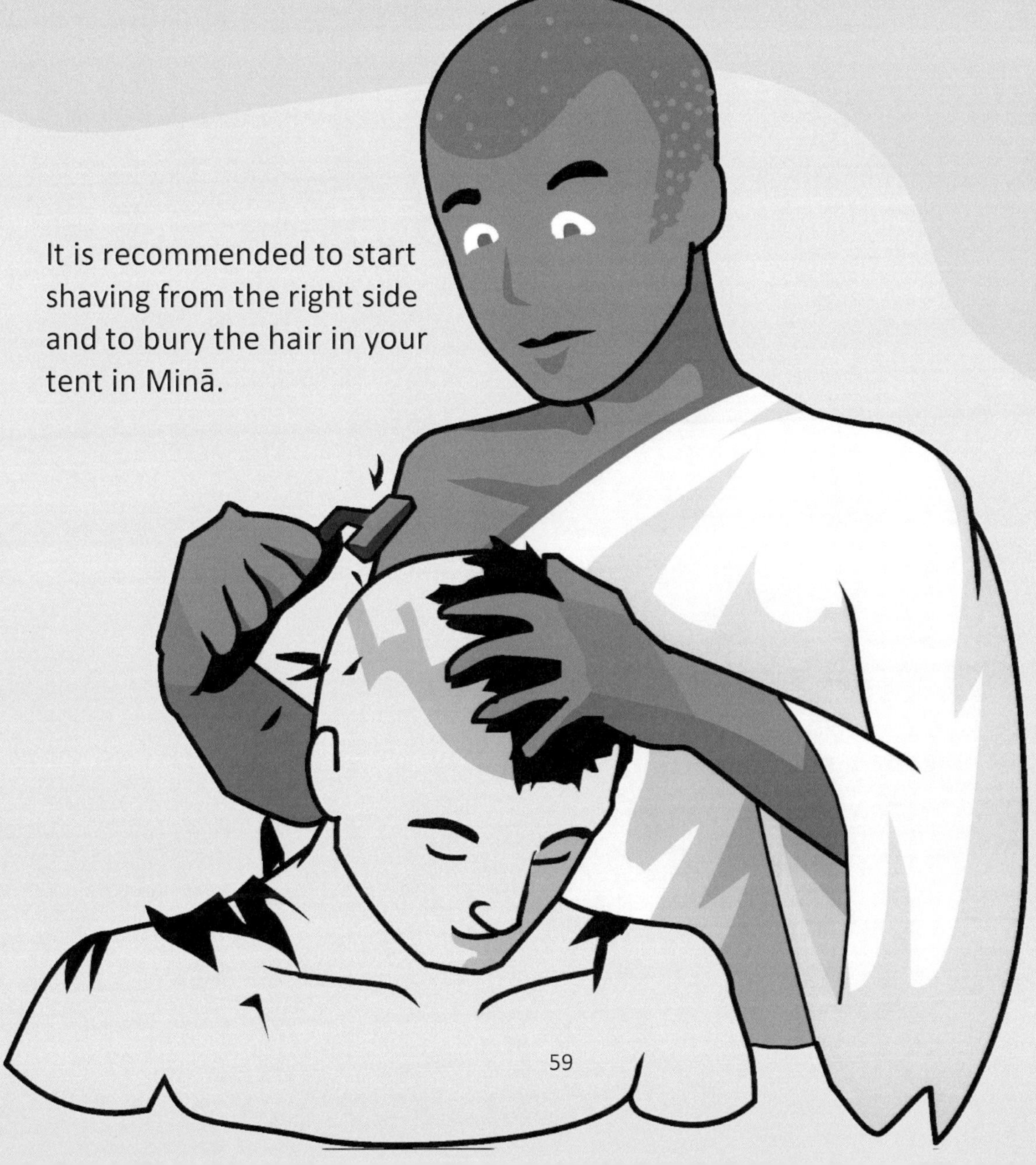

Mecca

- After performing *ḥalq* or *taqṣīr*, it is recommended to travel to Mecca and perform Ṭawāf al-Ḥajj, its prayer and the *Saʿy* on the 10th of Dhul-Ḥijjah.

- While these acts are obligatory, it is not required to do them immediately after the first rituals in Minā.

- If you choose to perform these acts on this day, you must return to the limits of Minā on the 11th night for your obligatory stay in Minā.

- The method and conditions for performing Ṭawāf al-Ḥajj, its prayer, and the *Saʿy* are the same as those described in ʿUmrah with the only difference being the intention. Refer to pages 30 to 37 for further details.

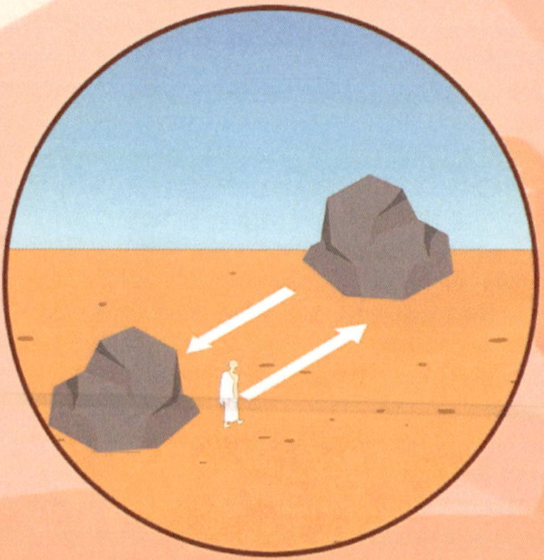

Make sure you return to Minā on the 11th night
Minā
Mecca
Muzdalifah
ʿArafah

Tawaf al-Nisa and its prayer

- Another obligation in Ḥajj al-Tamattuʿ is the performance of Ṭawāf al-Nisāʾ and its accompanying prayer. While both are mandatory, they are not pillars of Ḥajj, meaning that failing to perform them—whether intentionally or unintentionally—does not invalidate the Ḥajj.

- Ṭawāf al-Nisāʾ is obligatory for everyone: men, women, children, and even those who do not intend to marry. Although it is not a fundamental part of Ḥajj or ʿUmrah, the obligation remains, and it must be completed. If a pilgrim is unable to perform it, someone else must do it on their behalf.

- If a man neglects Ṭawāf al-Nisāʾ, women will remain prohibited for him, and similarly, if a woman neglects it, men will remain prohibited for her. For those performing Ḥajj as a proxy, they must perform Ṭawāf al-Nisāʾ for the person they represent, not for themselves.

- The method and conditions for Ṭawāf al-Nisāʾ and its prayer are the same as those for Ṭawāf al-Ḥajj and its prayer, with the only difference being the intention.

- Once a pilgrim completes Ṭawāf al-Nisāʾ and its prayer, marital relations become permissible. The main purpose of this *ṭawāf* is to lift the restriction on intimate relations after the state of *iḥrām*. If it is not performed, sexual relations remain prohibited, even after completing other Ḥajj rituals.

- This *ṭawāf* and its prayer can be performed in regular clothes, as long as it is done after *ḥalq* or *taqṣīr*. Additionally, it can be performed after your stay in Minā.

Tawaf al-Nisa and its prayer

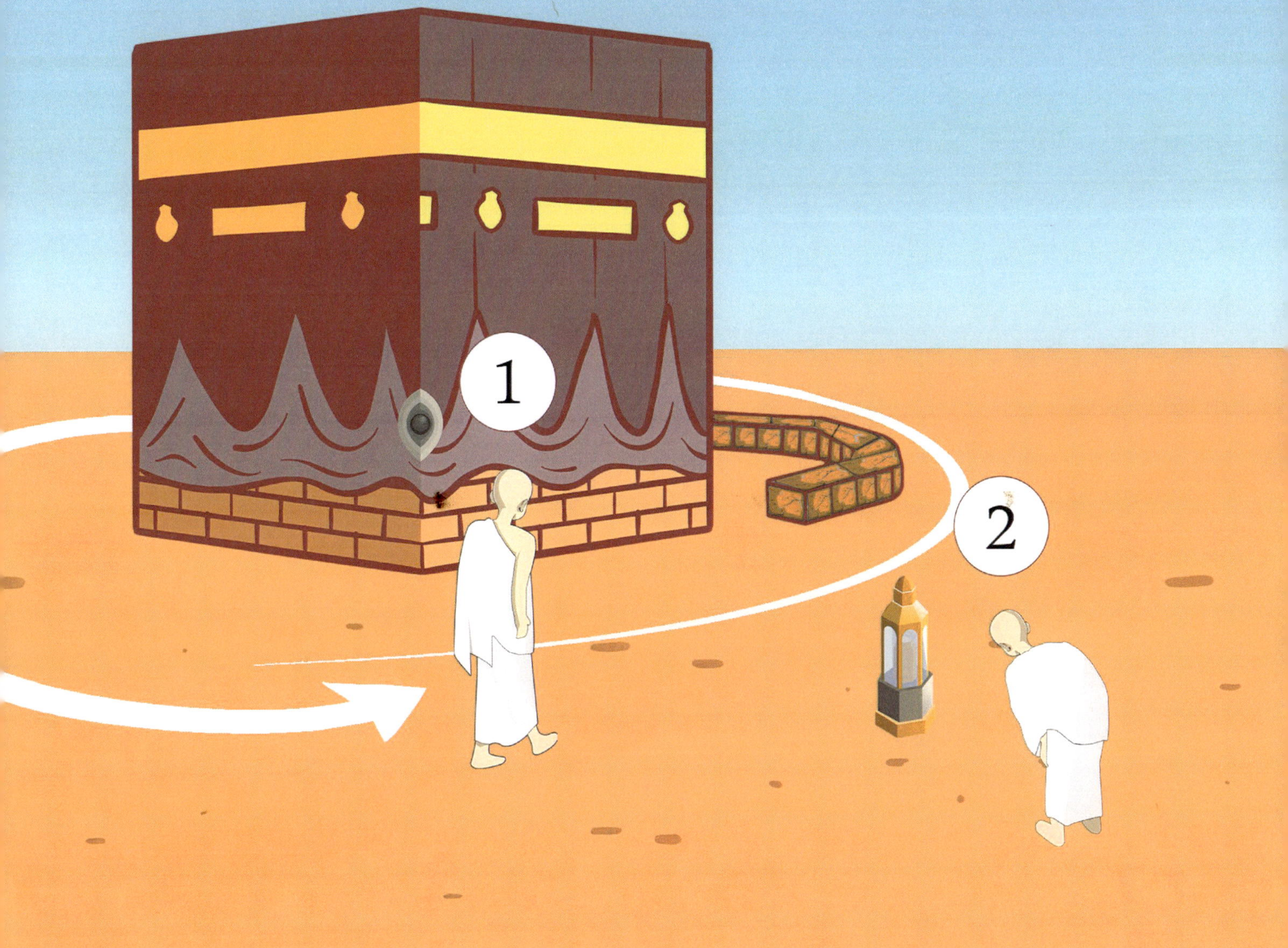

Continue your stay in Mina

- Our next obligatory ritual for Ḥajj al-Tamattuʿ is to stay in Minā on the nights of 11th and 12th of Dhul-Ḥijjah.
- If you went to Mecca and completed those acts mentioned earlier, you must return to Minā for your obligatory stay on the nights of the 11th and 12th.
- This act should be performed with the intention of seeking closeness to Allah ﷻ.
- On the 12th day, you may leave Minā after *Ẓuhr*. However, if you stay until *Maghrib*, you are required to remain for the night of the 13th until *Fajr* and perform the stoning ritual as well.
- It is not necessary to spend the entire night in Minā, you can choose to stay from sunset until midnight or from just before midnight until *Fajr*.
- During your stay, you must stone all three Jamarāt (the first, middle, and large pillars symbolising Satan) on both days between sunrise and sunset.

Minā

Stay in Minā on the 11th and 12th nights

Stoning all three Jamarat

- During your stay in Minā, the next obligatory ritual for Ḥajj al-Tamattuʿ is the stoning of the three Jamarāt (symbolising Satan), which includes the first, middle and Jamarah al-ʿAqabah (large pillar).

- You must carry out the stoning on the 11th and 12th of Dhul-Ḥijjah, and if you stay in Minā on the night of the 13th, it becomes obligatory to perform the stoning on the 13th as well.

- You must personally perform the stoning, as deputing someone else is not allowed unless you have a valid excuse.

- Start with the first pillar, then move to the middle one, and finally, complete the stoning with Jamarah al-ʿAqabah. If you do not follow this order, you will need to return and correct the sequence.

- If you are unable to perform the stoning yourself, such as due to illness, you should appoint someone to do it on your behalf. If your condition improves before the stoning period ends, it is obligatory as a precaution that you perform the stoning yourself as well.

- The same rules apply for stoning all three Jamarāt, as outlined previously for Jamarah al-ʿAqabah on page 54.

Stoning all three Jamarat

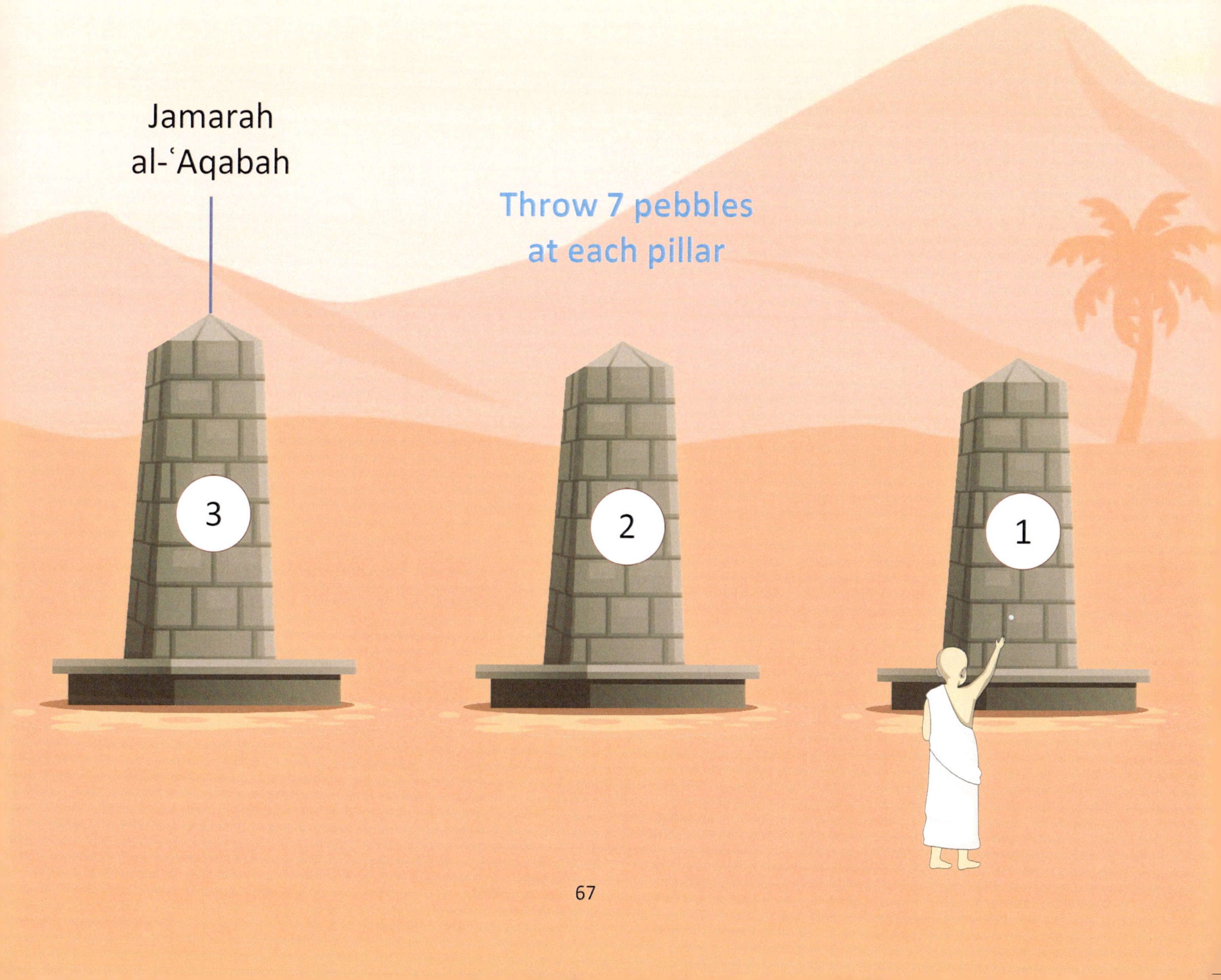

CONGRATULATIONS!

You have completed
Hajj al-Tammatu’

RECOMMENDED ACTS IN MECCA

Recommended acts in Mecca

- Be humble and respectful of the sanctity and significance of Mecca.
- Maintain a state of purity during your visit.
- Intend to perform good deeds, whether through prayer, charity or other acts of kindness.
- Frequent the remembrance of Allah ﷻ.
- Aim to complete the Qurān during your stay.
- Drink from the water of *Zamzam.*
- Gaze at the Kaʿbah often.
- Pray in each corner of the Kaʿbah.
- Perform a total of 360 *ṭawāfs* during your time in Mecca; if you cannot, then aim for 52 *ṭawāfs*; if that is also not possible, do what you can.
- Say *takbīr* three times upon exiting the Kaʿbah.

zamzam

Tawaf al-Wada'

- It is recommended for anyone wishing to leave Mecca to perform the farewell circumambulation (Ṭawāf al-Wadā'), touching the Black Stone and the *Yamānī* Corner in each round.

- At the end of the *ṭawāf*, it is *mustaḥab* to approach the Black Stone, cling to it, and offer praise to Allah ﷻ for His blessings and bounties. Afterward, send blessings upon the Prophet and his family.

- When leaving the Masjid al-Ḥarām, it is recommended to exit through the gate which faces the *Shāmī* Corner and pray for the opportunity to return again. Additionally, it is *mustaḥab* to purchase a *dirham's* worth of dates and give it in charity to the poor before departing.

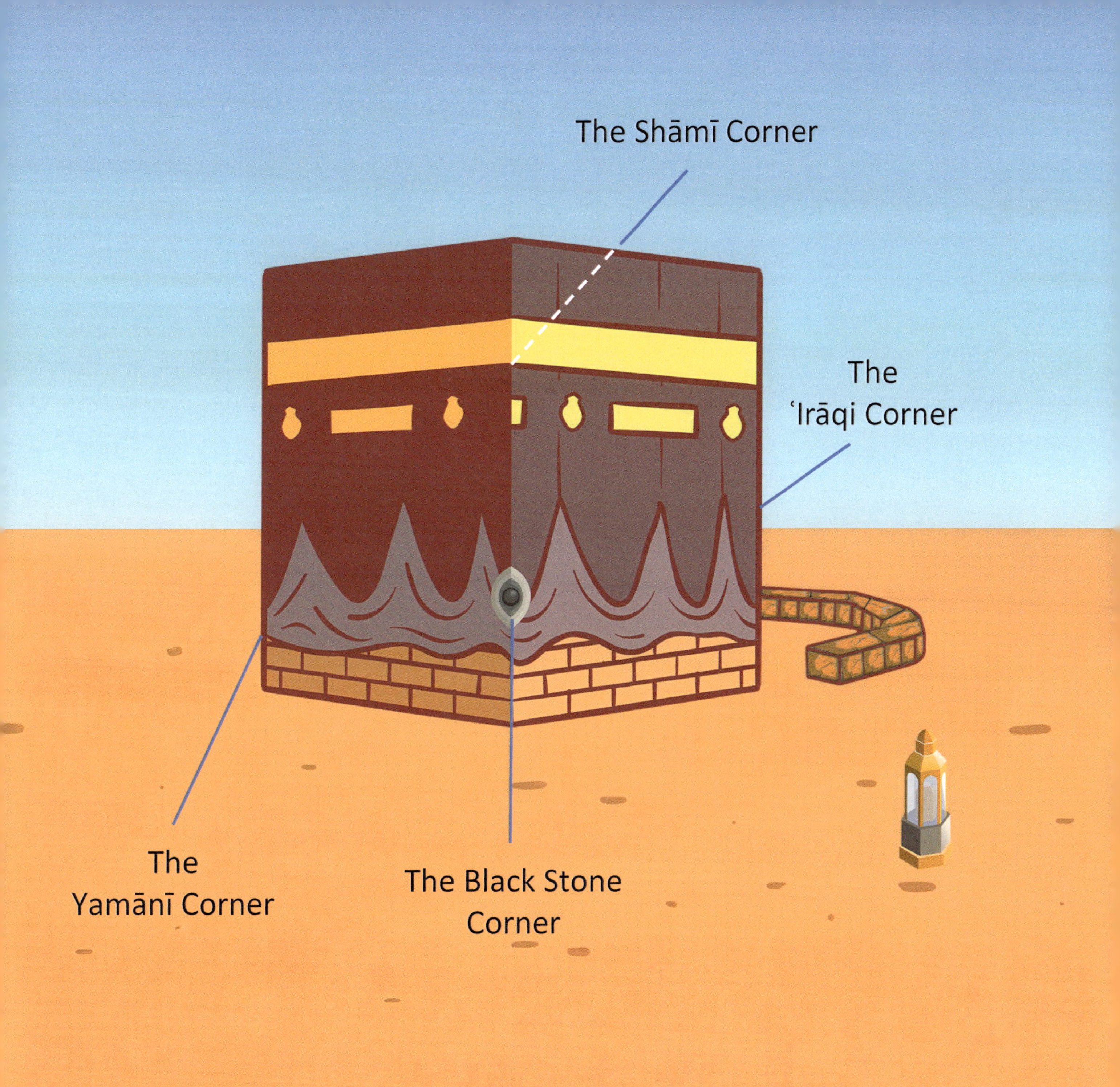
The Shāmī Corner
The
ʿIrāqi Corner
The
Yamānī Corner
The Black Stone
Corner

MEDINA

Medina

Visiting the Prophet Muḥammad ﷺ after Ḥajj is highly recommended and considered an essential extension of the spiritual journey. It signifies completing your pilgrimage with devotion to the Prophet ﷺ.

The journey to his shrine in Medina is viewed as an act of continued closeness to Allah ﷻ.

Imām al-Ṣādiq عليه السلام is reported to have said:
"When you perform Ḥajj and do not visit the Prophet, you have neglected a great right."
(*Man lā yaḥḍuruh al-Faqīh*)

This highlights the importance of the Prophet's visitation in achieving a spiritually fulfilling Ḥajj. Upon arrival, it is recommended to recite prayers asking for blessings upon the Prophet and his family.

Glossary

- *ʿAṣr* - Afternoon
- *Bab al-Salām* - The Gate of Peace
- *Dirham* - Unit of currency
- *Fajr* - Dawn
- *Ghusl* - Ritual wash
- *Ḥalāl* - Permissible
- *Ḥalq* - Shaving
- *Ḥarām* - Forbidden
- *Ḥaram* - Sacred precincts
- *Ḥijr Ismāʿīl* - The enclosure of Ismail
- *Idhkhir* - Aromatic grass
- *Iḥrām* - Enter a state of sanctity
- *ʿIrāqi Corner* - Corner that faces Iraq
- *Jamarāt* - Throwing stones at pillars
- *Janābah* - Major ritual impurity
- *Kaffārah* - Atonement
- *Khums* - Religious tax
- *Kuḥl* - Eye cosmetic
- *Maghrib* - Evening
- *Maqām Ibrāhīm* - Station of Abraham
- *Masjid al-Ḥarām* - The Sacred Mosque
- *Mount Raḥmah* - Mountain of Mercy
- *Muḥrim* - Entering the state of *iḥrām*
- *Mustaḥab* - Recommended
- *Qiblah* - Direction of prayer
- *Rakʿah* - Bowing
- *Saʿy* - To strive
- *Shāmī Corner* - Corner that faces Syria
- *Takbīr* - Allahu Akbar
- *Taqṣīr* - Trimming
- *Ṭawāf* - Circumambulation
- *Turbah* - Clay tablet for praying
- *Wuḍū* - Ablution
- *Yamānī Corner* - Corner that faces Yemen
- *Zakāh* - Charity
- *Zamzam* - Sacred water in Mecca
- *Ẓuhr* - Midday

Credit

All praise belongs to Allah, the All Merciful towards all existents, the Kindest towards believers. He Who has given us enough patience and courage to complete this book.

Islamic Lessons Made Easy would like to thank all those involved in this project for their hard work and commitment.

CREATOR
Abbas Ibrahim

EDITORS
Amir Hussein
Kawthar Ibrahim
Sheikh Dr Zaid Alsalami

اللَّهُمَّ صَلِّ عَلَى مُحَمَّدٍ وَآلِ مُحَمَّدٍ

Allahumma ṣalli ʿala Muḥammadi(n)w wa āli Muḥammad
O Allah, (please do) bless Muḥammad and the Household of Muḥammad

Contact: admin@islamiclessonsmadeeasy.com.au

Visit us:
Facebook.com/islamiclessonsmadeeasy
Youtube.com/islamiclessonsmadeeasy
Instagram.com/islamic_lessons_me
Islamiclessonsmadeeasy.com.au
Ilme.net.au

www.ingramcontent.com/pod-product-compliance
Lightning Source LLC
Chambersburg PA
CBRC091201070526
44583CB00008B/174

* 9 7 8 1 7 6 4 0 8 4 2 8 4 *